The Day
the Flowers Bloomed

Praise

With vibrant lyricism and precise imagery, Clara X. Roque-Wagner's debut collection, *The Day the Flowers Bloomed* sings off the page. Captured in dreamy and wondrous tones, weaving between English and Spanish, the poems are equal parts heartbreak and hope, leading us on a tender journey through love, healing, and the search for home. Roque-Wagner's words ache – "I reach for her arm but / it turns into cigarette smoke ash" and empower us – "I stand taller now with her name in my hands and her armor in my throat." This collection brims with self-discovery and growth, a resonant reminder of the importance of human connection and intimacy.
- Karo Ska, author of *Loving My Salt-drenched Bones*

Clara X. Roque-Wagner 's first poetry collection, *The Day the Flowers Bloomed* is beauty and pain lyrically woven through her storied poems. The Imagery is juxtaposed while each word feels perfectly composed and precisely placed. Her writing lulls you into a surreal reality where you don't want to wake from the word dreams.
-Gia Civerolo, author of
She Confuses Movies, Lovers, Angels and Poems.

Clara X. Roque-Wagner's poetry is a fairytale luring readers in with beauty and elegance, but does not shy away from life's difficult realities. It's a book of beauty, pain, healing, and ancestry that captures the heart of every reader. It's pure honesty will leave readers wanting more. -Hope

In *The Day the Flowers Bloomed*, Clara weaves a tapestry of her life through scenes adorned with exquisite, natural imagery. Each poem serves as a window into her world, capturing moments with such vividness that readers are effortlessly transported into her imagination. The way she intertwines her personal experiences with universal themes gives the sense that we, too, have lived through similar emotions and memories. Her words resonate on a deep, almost subconscious level, inviting us to reflect on our own journeys.This collection is not just a series of poems; it's an emotional experience. Clara's writing evokes a wide range of feelings, from joy and wonder to introspection and melancholy. For those who are attuned to the subtleties of life, this book will undoubtedly make you smile, think deeply, and perhaps even shed a tear or two. Her masterful use of imagery creates moments that linger in the mind long after the pages have been turned, leaving behind lessons and reflections that are hard to forget. Through her artful expression, Clara offers a glimpse into the beauty and complexity of life, making *The Day the Flowers Bloomed* a memorable and impactful read.
-Honey B. Rose

The Day
the Flowers Bloomed

Poems by

Clara X. Roque-Wagner

The Day the Flowers Bloomed
© 2024 Clara X. Roque-Wagner
ISBN: 979-8-9900531-9-9
Library of Congress Control Number:2024920190

Cover art:
© 2024, Clara X. Roque-Wagner

First Edition, 2024

Printed in the United States of America

Edited by Jay Lankau
Cover Design by Adam Martinez
Layout Design by Jessica S. Lin

I dedicate this book to the corners of my room for knowing who I am when I'm alone, to my grandmothers, Crispina Hernandez and Linda Wagner, for giving me the wisdom and courage I've always searched for, to my parents for gifting me this life, to the writers in my family that came before me but never got the chance to explore, and to my life partner Kris, thank you for making this house a home.

Aún no duermo y quién sabe por qué.

Será tal vez por el insomnio que se sienta en
mis hombros en estas noches tan oscuras.

O tal vez,

Es por la preocupación que entre nudos
amarra mi maldita mente
Dejándome sin aliento

Table of Contents

My Child Died the Day I Held Her

I was born on two feet,
my face burned and
my tears ached to swim in the river.
Mami held me in her veiny arms.
The hospital beds whispered.
> Copal sang from the walls.
> I was the seed
>> and she was
>>> such a long time ago.

I remember the way she smelled
like medicine, Calendula soap, tomato jam
> stuck to her gums.
Her hair grew dark and wirelike my fingers
> when they turned into weeds.
She became a fruit in my garden.
> Her leaves began to wilt.
> She was the moon in my arms
>> and I

>>> was the sun

a long time ago.

When the glass broke,
> my knees sunk into the ground
>> to clean up the mess that I made
> while my mother laughed and laughed.
I began to bleed from the inside.
> The sheets were my canvas.

I made art out of my spewing body
just to be told that this art isn't enough.
Under the lunar eclipse,
              that's where my mother's tenderness can
       be almost found.

Mami,
       why don't you braid my hair and
put flowers in the cracks of
              where my thoughts should be?
Mami, rest your palm on my heart

y persignate

como te enseñó mi abuela.
En el nombre del padre, del hijo
and to the milk of her breasts.
              They become an offering.

To the wolf that howls late at night,
       to the screams that echo
                     across cities and fields,
and to home,
where home is nothing more than a daydream.

I remember the way she smelled like
medicine and hospital beds

I remember the way
her little fingers would squeeze my thumb
and how warm my baby was.

But that was such a long time ago.

The Day the Flowers Bloomed

En estas manos me deshago de todos tus dolores.

The day you were born
was the day that the flowers bloomed.

I learned how to water the grass that day

and the roses,

      and the fig tree.

Years later, I watched you skip and run
and scrape your knee.
      Your hurt was mine
but always stronger.

I would swim through every ocean
      just to touch your face again.
I would show you how big the Earth is
      so that your eyes could also see
how much of it you've given me.

Let's sit between each continent.
      Let's count the stars.

      I named you after that one.

You are my light in the dark
when darkness looks for us.
      I'll save you.
You are the hands I raise.
I give you the veins from my wrists
and carry you home.

I can turn these mountains
　　　　into clouds for you,
　　　　　　　watch the river turn to rain,
watch the sun dissolve the moon.

I would cut my hair
just so I can give it all to you.

Florida Water

I place Florida Water on the window sill.
While the rain cries,
     the cemented wall is everything
                              I see.
I pour the water on my scalp,
               rub it in.
I'm thirsty.
            I think of leaving.
I fill up my brother's cup.
I wonder if he ever thinks of leaving too,
     of jumping through glass
just so he can fly to the moon

But

I think he likes it here.
I think he wants to stay.

I tell him a joke just to pass the time.
He laughs a little more than me.

How long has it been
            since I've heard my mother's voice?

I don't remember what she sounds like.

My brother and the dust around her

are the only ones that know her name.

Las Mañanitas

tell me,
how does this story end?
after the wolves howl
before the ocean hides one day.

take me
to a silent place
between here and there
as my furrowed brows
caress the wrinkles on my head.

jazz plays
through the window, incense burns,
I write about your sweet lips
when they kiss me.
I write about the moon.

look for me
behind a maple tree so that
I know to sing for you
the way you never did for me.

In Between Roses

I'm terrified of speaking
                       and to never be heard.

of hiding between the shadows
                 of yellow teeth
                       and coffee stains.
When you kiss me,
you taste just like the avenues I drive by.

The Earth falls at my feet
                       and I'm reminded why

this silence is so unbearable,

why I don't laugh as loud as I used to,

why the fruits in my mother's garden taste so bitter.

In between rose petals
                     and roses,

my tears still look the same
and I think about a life where
                       you never existed.

A life where my heartache becomes
a work of art
                       and my words
                   become my lesson.

...and the Day they Died

I thought of you yesterday when I planted plum seeds in
my garden,
                    as I was watering the grass
and plucking out the weeds in my home,
        I thought of you.
Mostly of your eyes and how afraid I am of them.
I thought of the way my body
                  swells at the sound of your voice.
I thought of
                  your teeth grinding against your lips
        when I made you this angry.
I thought of who you must've been
when you were my age.

                Was I ever in your dreams?

You should've braided your fingers in between my hair
so that I could recognize your touch more.

You should have swallowed your own tongue,
told me I was beautiful,
                a gift to you and Papi.

Was I ever in your dreams?

I fill my home with fruit and honey
                              to forget about you
and to forget about me
                  as your child.
Mango oozes down my chin.
                  I remember summers.
                  Blackberry picking,
                        The strings of the guitar.
                              You held my hand.
Remember?

        Or is it just another memory I've made up?

I dedicate my poetry to you
                  and dedicate my blood.

I bleed on this page
just so I can tell a story,
just so I can breathe again

Los Listones

Red is
the blood that
palpitates my uterus.

Yellow is
sour and bitter and
disappears in the winter.

Green reminds me of
sage stuck to your skin.

Orange is
the tree of childhood,
the branches became my arms and
the roots, my feet.

Blue is
just like the moon
when she sits so elegantly.

The ribbons in my hair are
my grandmothers.

They hold my aching body in
sweet moments like this,
when my toes play in the river
and my fingers count
the tadpoles swimming down
my ankles.

Let me drown in the current and
pretend to die so that
the ribbons rest
on my neck just a little longer.
I land in between
the abyss of somewhere
and nowhere.

The wires that spill from my head
turn my mind into water.
The sky tastes just
like persimmons and
my tongue tingles when
I lick its center.

Without my veins pulsating,
I don't know how
to breathe.
I spread apricot jam on
my wounds and my skin
almost heals.

My grandmothers
taught themselves to smile
picking the weeds out from
underneath me,
sweeping bougainvillea petals
off the ground.

My grandmothers
taught me how to smile.
They also taught me how
to pray
and taught me how
not to.

It Rained Roses Last Summer

It rained roses last summer.
I still have the photographs you took of me.
My arms, reaching for disappearance.
Children go missing and I still don't know where to find
you.

Your cheek spreads onto mine like butter.

Every day I think about stripping myself from all the
violence in between my skin
when yours is rich and mine,
una cosecha,
buscando frutas entre mis yerbas.

This battle looks like art.

The chest I've hid from you has taught me patience,
while there has been no remedy for losing every vein
I've ever held onto.
We feed from the moisture of our elbows.

Love is the color of subconsciousness.

Our fight grows.
We choose this pattern of creating pain from something
beautiful.
Believing that my feet are only guiding me to meet the
sun.

We've built this mountain in between us.
And I've forgotten how to climb.

You stole my voice when I spoke about

time being invisible.

I rescued the flowers stemming from my mouth
and you shrink.
I lay beside you.

I drown in silence.

We swim in waters deeper than the sky.
We fly in every direction.
We give ourselves the role of bending backwards and
forwards.
Forwards and backwards
for the sake of drinking ourselves to sleep.

I'm afraid to hold your hand.

To eat the soil from my own backyard.
To rub away at the calluses on my hands.
To search for my mind in the ocean

To never know what I'm looking for.

Bougainvilleas

She smells like eucalyptus and sage on her loneliest
nights.

When the sun is asleep, she dreams of seeing a world
where
      money is not the devil

and bodies like hers and mine are worshiped
                             and honored
because

aren't we deserving of that?

I tell her just to lie with me here for a second

      until the sheets swallow us
and we cease to exist.

The Earth would be so much quieter if it was just the
two of us.

I wake up in the morning with incense on my breath,
                reminiscing

on the days where we would sing to the moon, laugh
until we almost choked on our own saliva,
when we would hold each other's hands.

Her shoulder was the perfect place for my head to land
on.

I thought to myself that one day I would marry her.

That we would celebrate a love that was dug from the
soil that raised us
                    and then watched us bloom.

Our gray hairs spill onto the bed.

Her eyes remind me of an ocean I've drowned in.

The creases on our faces are deeper than we care to
know.

The wrinkles around our lips tell the story of age
and somehow,
        she's even more beautiful than before.

I still dream of Sundays.

Cafecito poured into little cups from
once   upon   a time.

Lavender stains my tongue.

Bougainvillea petals paint the backyard.

She smiles at me again.

I reach for her arm but
it turns into cigarette smoke ash.

All I'm left with is just the memory

of her.

La Mano Santa

Escucho los cantos de la sala
mientras pico la cebolla
y empiezan a bailar.

Pongo el chile en la sartén.
Mi piel y los sentidos,
arden igual que el aceite.

Nadie me enseñó a cocinar.
Con las venas de mis dedos,
todo se aprende.

Pienso en el coraje y la decepción.
El jugo del tomate peina
los pelos de mis brazos.

El ajo sabe a cuentos
que la luz ya me ha contado.
Me dicen que llevo la mano santa.

Entre cada sabor,
me acuerdo de esa casa donde
corre el antepasado.

De repente, se queman las tortillas.
Le pido a la hoja santa
que me ayude a olvidar.

I'll Remember You in This Home

I wonder why these thoughts are so familiar.

>They look like memories
>but feel like dreams.

>I see a child play and she waves
>goodbye to me.

>>She looks like someone I knew.

I look around my home.

This house is filled with children's bodies.

>I boil water for tea

>>to sit here a while.

I hope that when the sun
takes me away,

I'll remember

you

                                         in this home

sitting by the window,
sipping on your tea,
smiling at the neighbors.

They know you like the roses on the porch do.
They know you like the cries I've never heard.

They know you the way I'll never know myself.

Your body lives here.

How do I grieve somebody I don't know?

Willow Tree

There's a child that lives in a willow tree.

At night, when she sleeps, she thinks about the home she left and it almost feels forgotten. The white walls and the decorated curtains swallowed each day like there was never a tomorrow.

Here, she reimagines herself as a hummingbird.

Like the one she knew
a long, long time ago.

The hummingbird became her friend because they understood each other. And they laughed. And they sang together. And the hummingbird convinced the child to fly away.

"Will I ever be back?"
"Only if you want to be,"
said the hummingbird.

Now, all the child does is dream.

She dreams of swimming in the middle of the ocean and digging her fingernails into the sand and drowning so that she could live there forever.
She dreams of wearing butterflies in her hair so that the Earth will see her as something beautiful. She dreams of flying away again. Where the abyss is an empty place between here and there.

Her body burns
and the wind never finds her.

Her body turns to ash
and her mother never looks for her.

The leaves become her sisters and the roots of
the tree are the ancestors who dance under the moon
until the angels fall.

The child screams and her screams almost save
her. Her face slowly disappears and I think that one day
no one will ever remember her.

Casa

I escape my mother's house with nothing but skin. I close my eyes and begin to run to where the sky and the ocean meet for the very first time. If I ask politely, will they allow me to live there? To build a home between the ripples and the sun? I'm far enough now to where my yells and screams won't save me. I needed to be saved a long time ago.

Casa II

I was found underneath an orange tree. I had forgotten how to walk, let alone swim and run. The weight of the tears I carry makes it seem like I'm drowning all of the time. My naked body is covered in thorns. I think about going back home to my mother. Maybe she'll be able to lick the salt off my wounds for once.

If Plums Could Talk

How many birds sit in an apple tree and sing?
How many of them have lost their feathers?

The years fall from the clouds and I watch them disap-
pear.
I make a promise to myself to never cry.
But
I've never known a promise I could keep.

When the woman laughs, she tells a story through her
aging teeth.
Wine bleeds from her veins,
the ceiling collapses,
and she is no longer able to escape her screams.

She laughs louder than before.
Her screech rings in my ear
like when a bullet
caresses your cheek.

How many angels die in fear?
How many of them remember Earth
when Earth was only land?

The mirror looks me in the eyes and reminds me
that my hands were never mine to begin with.
That my feet belonged to somebody else.

When I try to run,
the woman laughs for hours
and hours
until her breath leaves her body.

Wine bleeds from her veins,
the ceiling collapses.
This time she cries louder than
when the mountains used to watch her scream.

I've dreamt of a home where plums could talk.
A home where the fern leaves always listened.
Where my mother was as soft as silk.
I was only a child being put to sleep.

How long until she's forgiven?
How long until she's forgiven me?

Canto

Can I sing to you in whispers?
The hums in my head spill like
blood on my cheek,
like tears.

"Use your tongue to speak, cabrona."

My own silence drowns me.

My throat is coated with wax
from the candles I burn on my altar.
The ancestors starve and
I hear their voices sing to me

They get louder and
                            louder

and I fly away with them.

Our land was stolen a long time ago
but the birds and the flowers still live here

                            and I still sing

along with them.

Years of Silence

I got my breath taken from me before I really learned
how to swim.The day that my voice drowned, I told
myself that I don't live here anymore,
                    or that I don't know how to live.

I learned that laughter was a sacred thing that
belonged to only children. But when I was a child,
I never really sang, or laughed, or
                              put myself to sleep.

I closed my eyes just to see a different body,
just to hear a different voice. I pictured myself running
barefoot through the woods,
going anywhere away from here.

and she jumped
to reach the clouds
and she swayed with them
and she rested
and she never learned to say
"I love you,"
                    not even to her parents
                    or her siblings

or to the hills that watched her grow.

Her eyes began to know of heartbreak and
her veins trapped her through
                    years and years
                                and years and years

and years
of silence.

Mockingbird

Someone told me a story once
about a mockingbird who lost her voice.

She lost it somewhere in the mountains.
How it happened is still a question I ask.

The poor mockingbird lived the rest of her life trying to
rescue it.

No matter how many oceans she crossed, she was never
able to sing again.

Now, when you close your eyes and listen closely to the
sounds of the hills, you can hear her cry;

'tierra mia, regalame tu aliento...aconséjame qué hacer
con este corazón que está muerto de hambre...'

I tell my children this same old tale.
A mockingbird who can not mock is just a bird without
its wings.

This House is Not a Home

If I ever touch the sun, would it hurt as much as this?

I have nowhere to go.

       This house is not a home without you, Love.

I look for you in different corners of this planet we call ours,
       but I can never find you.

This house is not a home.

       Please come home.

I miss your golden skin and how it shined
even when it rained.

       I miss the cigarette smoke on your breath,

I miss waking up before you so that I could rub your
face in oils.

I miss your eyelids and the way my lips land
                                    so perfectly.

Maybe if I cry a little louder,
                    you'll finally hear me.

          Hold me and remind me.

Why should I stay?

Ombligo

It's quiet on this side of the world.
            I hold my palms up towards the branches
and call them by their names.
            I howl to the waters
and the creek remembers me.

The trees welcome my body
                        like my body never left,
as a sparkle in my mother's eye,
                        as a seed sprouting.

My umbilical cord is buried here.
            I wrap it around my wrist
            like a bracelet,
                  like the chains that hold me still.

Aquí siguen mis difuntos
                  on the land that raised them.
I sweep the dirt off the patio.
                  This is where my children live.
I bury their belly buttons right beneath my own

para que la soledad no nos gane,

para aprender a vivir sin ellos.

Los Vientos

Maybe it was wrong of me to think
that everything would still be the same.
People in their canvas painted homes.
Los gritos de los escuincles but
my voice is swallowed by the rooster.
I think that's why he won't
let me sleep.
En mi casa ya no llegan los vientos.
Se ocultan las palabras.
Las culebras ya no vienen
y sus corazones ya no tienen
para que vivir.

Mezcal

Papi paints mezcal on my gums
        so that by the time I grow up,
I know how to cure a broken heart.
                I lick the salt off the rim,
                    take a sip of boiling water,
I think about how white the walls are.
Maybe in another life they would be a different color.

Church Bells

I can just about count each star while
the Azucenas sleep,
the sky looks almost translucent
and I came to offer my heart.

I look for places where
my mother is the land,
my father, the root,
where their mothers and their fathers
are the seeds planted a long time ago.

Our footsteps walk barefoot on a road
that will always remember us.
We are its children.
Our parents turn their callus
into armor.
Roses bloomed from that.

We make our way down the road,
to the church that raised us somehow.
With mezcal on our chins
and the Agave plant at our fingertips,
everybody knows our name.

I carved a heart on my wrist once.
My blood stained the pavement.
The thorn disappeared into my veins.

As we stand around the saints of
our past,
I think about how beautiful
life can be when
we play together like
we used to as kids.

My grandmother meets us in the doorway.
I give her a kiss on the cheek.
Her body fades again
and the church bells ring.

Goodbye to the Petals

Maybe,
I've outgrown the trees
      and the dirt roads,
      and the children I once knew
            aren't children anymore.

The jokes I tell don't make anybody laugh.
When my grandmother was buried, the distance be-
tween me and this Earth grew further away.
For lots of days I cried,
but there were also a lot of days
      I danced and
            ran around the bushes
            and rested in the creek.

The sun felt warm around my shoulders
as he kissed me goodnight.
That was the last day I saw him.

Things are different now.
This place is magical but I think
                        I no longer believe in it.
Even as I'm surrounded by the bougainvillea petals,
the beauty on the horizon
                        still seems so far away.

Esperanza

In English my name means 'hope.' In Spanish, it rolls
off the tongue like piloncillo in the evenings,
like café de olla. Ay, cómo se me antoja, to sit in my
grandmother's bright pink kitchen, pans and coffee
mugs and leftover beans on the stove. The walls al-
most blind me. I can still feel the raspiness of her voice
against my skin. I'm there for hours as she tells me the
same old story she's always told. When her husband
left the first time, she wasn't sure if he'd ever return.
He gifted her six children so that she would never feel
alone but in the end, she died of loneliness.

My name is Esperanza and I was named after her.
Esperanza means things like sadness and waiting.
It means the color brown. My name is Mexican records
on Sunday mornings. Songs like sobbing, songs like
yearning and songs of love. In school, they always say
my name funny, like the syllables hurt the roofs of
their mouths. In Spanish, my name is made up of softer
things, things like gold and things like satin. I prefer my
name that way. The way my grandmother wore hers like
jewels around her neck, around her ankles and wrists.
Her name stung you every time she spoke. I stand taller
now with her name in my hands and her armor in my
throat.

It Was Never Mine to Keep

The way that my name stumbled
through her teeth and
          slid down her lips
was as if this was the first time
she'd ever said it.
          It sounded harsh
                    and tasted sour.

She's taken my name with her
          and has made it her own.
Each letter chewed
                    and spit back up.
She sits on this platter
          waiting
           to be enjoyed by guests.

The dress I wear is
just the right amount of elegance
for this occasion.
My hair is adorned
with burnt ribbons
the same color I wore
the day I was born.

I put feathers in my ears and
my hands feel as light as the wind.
		I grab the clouds just to hold them.
				To remember that I stand this tall.
For these unrequited walls
to let me fly again.

The rosary hangs from my altar,
says goodbye and
		that's when I know
		it's time for me to leave.
With a mecate tied around my waist,
I begin to walk
through fields,
mountains, oceans.
				I come up for air.

I don't know where to go
but to touch the moon,
that has always been my dream.
To engrave each letter of my name
		in a different corner

           so they're never found together.
      Or all at once.

I gift myself back to the Earth
and the name I thought I owned
is given back to my mother.

It was never mine to keep.

El Cielo a Mis Pies

me canso de tanto

                                         pensar

mi mente

        llora

y   ruega

y   perdona

mi nombre

        ya no sale de su jaula

        la lumbre del cigarro

                              huele a mi alma

humo y viento

ya no se con cual pulmón respirar

es el desahogo de las nubes

                              es el cielo a mis pies

las montañas se enredan entre

                      camino

                           e

                                  historia

mi vieja carga el sol

carga el mundo

                en cada hombro

le toco su piel   y

yo tambien

                    me voy de aquí

con el viento sigo volando

Body

I lie awake until the ribbons in my hair
recite this poem.

They're not here to watch me bleed.

My breasts exaggerate their grins when
a man calls me pretty.

My own flesh begins to eat itself.

I'm reminded that this body isn't mine

and never was to begin with.

Silverware

My head is wrapped in VapoRub

Sage

Eucalyptus.

I can't tell if this is sweat
or if it's only tears.
I hear my mother's weeping
from the other room.

I know better than to cure a broken heart.

The table is set with
gold silverware
plastic cups
tiny plates
from a long, long time ago.
the placemats are overused,
the centerpiece holds my fingers.

My fingers get stuck.

I'm served carrots,
burnt beans, and rice.
I swallow my food like
it's the last meal on Earth.
The minutes on the clock say
that this is the last time
I'll ever sit here

but I know that's not true.

I don't recognize these walls
or the roof above me
or the paintings on the mantel
or how it always feels so cold,
even in the summer.

My tongue is paralyzed again.

Through these open doors
lies a body that's been left empty.

A body lies
and I never learn to speak.

Curandera

The aloe vera plant cures the scabs on your skin
just like when the sun cures the moon
on the nights she cries,
like the way my eyes and mouth go together
like cinnamon and milk.

I'm stuck between

carcajadas sabrosas
            and palabras.

A woman on the train tells me that I'm the most beauti-
ful person she's ever seen.
I show her the cuts on my lips
and my dirty teeth
and my fingernails that need trimming.

The woman smiles at me.

She gets off the train.

I never see her again

but I think about her every day.

This life makes no more sense to me.
I begged the world to choose me,
I bent my knees and prayed and
now that I'm here,
I want nothing more
than to leave.

Empty Fields

Afternoons felt longer.
As the sun set behind the hills,
tomorrow would never come.

My breath began to feel like
it was running out of time.
I remember the first time I tasted her spit,
my palms gripping onto the sheets, my legs tying them-
selves to the bed.

The days grew longer,
heavier and
even if I ever went away,
her tenderness was everything I knew.

You're the reason for this void,
for this empty field,
for how painful it is to breathe,
for the cracks in the wall,

My body is a painting.
There's fungus growing from
the tips of my hair,
my life is a tree closer to dying than
to living and suddenly,

I forgot how to speak.

The Magnolia Tree Blossoms

I don't know when the last time was
                that my body was invisible.

That person over there looks just like me
and for once,

                Mami calls me pretty.

I'm compared to a Magnolia tree in the spring.

                My body is here

and for once,

that's all that matters.

Mar

How many days are left on Earth?
What if I take a spaceship to the moon?
Could I live there?

My braids are long enough to kiss the sand.
They remind me of an ocean.

But I'm afraid of oceans.

Your blue eyes stain my skin.

A knife chops my hair and
drowns me with it.

I wonder if I'll live this time.

El Sueño de Mil Noches

Pasaron mil noches.
Estrellas empapadas en mis lágrimas.
Risas sabrosas que me ahogaban.

I wrote about you
long before I knew you.

I dreamt about you
long before

I knew you.

Daydream

I daydream of
a home with a garden
where our fingers dig.

I kiss the dirt between your nails.

Our imagination blooms
and gives us sunflowers.

This is now my favorite season.

Let me nourish you with bowls of fruit.

papaya
     mango

               sandía

I lick the lemon off your tongue.
Your lips are sweet like honey.

When the Stars Disappear

we look up,

   just to stare at the moon.

how she glistens and
       yawns

there is nothing in the air but

   distance.

the river murmurs
   a lovely sound.

the sound rings in my ear

until

I can no longer hear the
       crickets chirp.

the sweetness of
      your lips
     intertwine
      with mine.
tonight,
   there are no more stars in the sky
or clouds.

I sit in between your legs,
against your chest.

I can feel your heartbeat

like it's brushing my hair.

I've forgotten every thought that has ever
                                            led me here

to you.

my fingers
        through yours.

I almost told you that I love you.

You became the home I saw in my sleep.

Un Puño de Tierra

At the end of life,
the body I've created for myself
turns to dust, air,
and almost nothing.

I'm afraid to die.

I'm afraid that I will leave this land
the same way I came,
with blood on my scalp
and a sheet that covers me up
to my belly button.

The only thing I seem to think about is,
what would happen to us?
I remember the day we met so clearly.
It was like,
"This is where
I'm supposed to be."
You offered me a cigarette and
that's as close as I came to
breathing that night.

 You've made me more afraid to die.
Could you live without me?

To die is to be nowhere but anywhere,
It's to laugh and to cry,
to disappear into the heart of the Earth,
it's to have nothing left.

This is where I want to stay.
Until the bougainvillea tree

stops blooming,
Until my umbilical cord
is dug up,
until the only thing I leave with
is a fistfull of rocks.

The Morning My Father Screamed

Can I lie in your bed for a while?
Just until the sun rises in the morning.
Maybe that's when I'll remember your voice.
I lie beneath the blankets and I hear the phone ring.

Mama, is it really you?
The last time we spoke was in my dream.
I didn't know that you were dead yet.
Until I held my breath and heard my father scream.

Mosquita Mía

Ayer me visitó la muerte.

> Fue en esa esquina,
> donde bebió la leche de los encantos.
> Ella me buscó entre cada camino.

> Allí,
> en esa esquina,
> la muerte tragó y tragó.

> En esa esquina,
> fue que la muerte me encontró.

En su cuerpo carga el ojo del '¿quién será?'
Sus colores rinden con el viento
y amanecen con la amargura del sol.
La muerte se parece a la mosca
que descansa en mi pasillo.

Mosquita,
atrévete a volar entre fuego y humo,
a salvar mis penas,
a engañar a los viejos
que sigan esta lucha.
Protégeme del mal.

Mosquita mía,
cuida a mi papi cuando llora por ti.
Ruégale a mi madre
que ya no se esconda.
Ni entre cada labio.
Ni entre cada diente.

Mosquita,
jalame de la hierbas
y deja de soñar.
Diles que la vida sigue contando
aunque uno ya no sepa contar.

Mosquita mía,
regalame tu vida.

The Azucena flowers bloom.
The river is filled with tadpoles.
My grandmother's shiny,
crinkly fingers are in the shape of a cross.
En el nombre del padre, del hijo, y del espíritu santo.
I peck the tip of her thumb.
Amen.

Author Bio

Clara Ximena Roque-Wagner is a multimedia artist and writer who grew up in the Bay Area. Though she enjoys spending her free time working on creative projects, she has always had a passion for writing. Clara received a B.A in Creative Writing from San Francisco State University in 2021, and had her work featured in issues of the school's *Transfer Magazine*. Clara's other published works include *La Receta Del Mole* which can be found on the online literary magazine *Sad Girl Diaries* and her zine *Cafe con Leche*. You can find her at her local coffee shop sipping on her *cafecito* and writing about the world's playground.

Publishers Note

Daxson publishing was created to help marginalized artists publish their work, so the world can hear their voice. The vision for this publishing house is to help people get their work out there, and not have them struggle finding their way through the publishing process. Everyone's voice deserves to be heard, and we are here to help. If you are interested in submitting a manuscript, email daxsonpublishing@gmail.com.

www.ingramcontent.com/pod-product-compliance
Lightning Source LLC
Chambersburg PA
CBHW051330120626
46547CB00016B/2482